THE FOX FAMILY GENEALOGY

By
Katherine Fletcher

THE FOX FAMILY

GENERATION ONE
Charles Fox and Eunice Matthews

Eunice Matthews Fox
Born March 11, 1894 in Barnwell
County, SC and died Jan 10, 1982 in SC.
Parents: William Christian Matthews
(1848-1903) and
Mary Elizabeth Johnston Matthews
(1860-1909)
Spouse: Charlie Fox (1883-1953) and
children:
William Anderson Fox (1920-1987)
William M. Fox (1930-1998)
Siblings: Annie Matthews Dodenhoff
(1889-1964)
Matt Lott Matthews (1895-1944)
buried oak grove Baptist church
cemetery in Batesburg, Lexington
County, SC.

CHARLES FOX

Born March 18, 1883 and died on July
31, 1953 mother is listed as Amanda
Watkins fox
Spouses: Florence Williamson Fox
(1883-1919) and Eunice Matthews Fox
(1894-1982)

Children:
  Charlie Bruce Fox (1910 - 1970)*
  Ashton Heyman Fox (1911 - 1967)*
  Geneva Fox Maddox (1914 - 2005)*
  William Anderson Fox (1920 - 1987)*
  William M Fox (1930 - 1998)*

Siblings:
  Georgia Fox Hall (1874 - 1949)*
  James Southern Fox (1877 - 1944)*
  Charlie Fox (1883 - 1953)
  Lawrence M. Fox (1889 - 1945)*
  Clifton Clarence Fox (1890 - 1941)*
  Daniel Elbert Fox (1902 - 1962)*

Estelle Fox Irick (1904 - 1967)*
Lottie Ellen Fox Waites (1905 - 1999)*
Theodore Claude Fox (1907 - 1989)*
Joseph Blease Fox (1911 - 1983)*

Rites Held For C. Fox

Funeral services for Charlie Fox 70, of Aiken, Rt. 4, were held at Oak Grove Baptist church yesterday at 4 p. m., with the Rev. Jack M. Corry and Rev. J. Yates Frady officiating. Interment followed in the church cemetery.

Mr. Fox, a lifelong resident of Aiken county, was a well known farmer. He was a member of Old Kedron Baptist church. He had been in failing health for some months and seriously ill for a week.

Immediate survivors include his wife, Mrs. Eunice Matthews Fox; four daughters. Mrs. Vernon Maddox of North Augusta; Mrs. J. H. Corley of Gary. Ind., Miss Mandy Fox and Miss Jane Fox, both of Augusta; six sons, Bruce Fox of Graniteville, Ashton H. and Anderson Fox, both of Aiken, Carl Fox of Orangeburg, Ralph Fox of Aiken, Rt. 4, and Bill Fox, U. S. Navy, USS Wyoming; two half-sisters, Mrs. E. B. Waites of Aiken, and Mrs. L. M. Irick of Warrenville; and two brothers, Watson Fox of Batesburg, and Phoenix Fox of Aiken; three half-brothers, Daniel, Theodore, and Blease Fox all of Aiken.

GENERATION TWO

Southern Fox (1853)1913) born in
Lexington, SC and Frances Laura Pink
Williamson & Julia Hall Fox
There is a discrepancy saying that
Amanda Watkins Fox is Charlie Fox's
mother
Birth: Feb. 2, 1853
South Carolina, USA
Death: May 17, 1913

Family links:
Parents:
 Melison or Michael Watson Fox (1822
- 1869)

Spouses:
 Frances Laura Pink Williamson Fox
(1853 - 1900)*
 Julia Hall Fox (1872 - 1950)*

Children:
 Georgia Fox Hall (1874 - 1949)*
 James Southern Fox (1877 - 1944)*
 Charlie Fox (1883 - 1953)*
 Lawrence M. Fox (1889 - 1945)*

Clifton Clarence Fox (1890 - 1941)*
Daniel Elbert Fox (1902 - 1962)*
Estelle Fox Irick (1904 - 1967)*
Lottie Ellen Fox Waites (1905 - 1999)*
Theodore Claude Fox (1907 - 1989)*
Joseph Blease Fox (1911 - 1983)*

Siblings:
John Sidney Fox (1845 - 1881)*
Henrietta Fox Jones (1848 - 1925)*
Southern Fox (1853 - 1913)
Pope Butler Fox (1854 - 1921)*
Felix Fox (1856 - 1916)*
Michael Watson Fox (1858 - 1928)*

GENERATION THREE

Melison or Michael Watson Fox (1822-1869) and Almirah Herron (1828-)

Birth: Dec. 5, 1822, USA
Richland County, SC
Death: Jan. 12, 1869 SC
South Carolina, USA

Family links:

Children:
  John Sidney Fox (1845 - 1881)*
  Henrietta Fox Jones (1848 - 1925)*
  Southern Fox (1853 - 1913)*
  Pope Butler Fox (1854 - 1921)*
  Felix Fox (1856 - 1916)*
  Michael Watson Fox (1858 - 1928)*

*Calculated relationship

Burial:
Mount Ebal Baptist Church Cemetery
Aiken County
South Carolina, USA

GENERATION FOUR

Thomas Fox (1770-1845) and Sarah
Sallie Barton (1784-1825)

GENERATION FIVE

Thomas Fox (1725 NC to 1822
Orangeburg, SC) and Elizabeth
Hancock

GENREATION SIX

Henry Fox III (1698-1770) and Mary
Goodwyn (1698-1745)

Born in Surrey Co, VA and died in
Craven , SC.

Married Martha Keen and had William,
Joseph. Married Mary Goodwyn and
had Unity, Thomas, John.

GENERATION SEVEN

Henry Fox II (1674-1750) and Mary
Kendrick (1678-1704)

born in New Kent, VA and died in
Brunswick VA.

GENREATION EIGHT

Henry Fox (1650-1714) and Anne West (1655-1708)

Also married to Mary Claiborne.

Henry was born in King William, Surrey Co, VA and died same place.

Henry Fox son of John Fox who was a ship captain and trader. Henry Fox was a member of St. John's parish in 1695 and in 1699 was a court justice. In 1710, he was a member of the house of burgesses. With his wife, Anne, daughter of Colonel John West, he had several sons, John, Thomas and Henry Fox.

Anne's grandfather was Governor John West and the fifth son of the second Lord Delaware and Anne, the daughter of Sir Thomas Knellys (first cousin to Queen Elizabeth (1533-1603).

** I found a reference that says the descendants of Henry and Anne have blood of Henry III (1207) and Edward the first (1239) from the Royal house of

Plantagenet.   This includes Louis the lion and William the Conqueror.

I find mention of Colonel Norwood in this war and also his being wounded in the royal service, thus:

"And here (at the seige of Bristol, July 1643) Captain Henry Norwood, a volunteer under Colonel Washington, having charged in among them (the Roundheads) was shot in the face with powder by the enemy's captain, whom in recompense he killed upon the place."

Those Foxes who spring from the union of Henry Fox and Anne West have, in their veins, through the Wests, the blood of Henry III (1207-1272), Edward I (1239-1307), "by far the ablest of all the Kings of the House of Plantagenet," Edward III (1313-1377), the father of the Black Prince, and Louis VIII, of France (1223-1226), called Louis le Lion, he being, also, the father of St. Louis, and are, in consequence, really descendants of William the Conqueror (1027-1087). And yet, this is a circumstance of birth which must be regarded as of only a certain weight, for the same distinction is, in one of the above cases, shared by five thousand moderns, and, in another, by twenty thousand; in fact, I have been surprised to find how very many people are descended from royalty, as might very properly and legitimately be the fact through younger sons, non-regnant, as in these Fox instances. Further, Governor John West, the grandfather of Anne West, was the fifth son of the second Lord Delaware and Anne, the daughter of Sir Thomas Knollys, K. G., by Catherine Cary, first cousin of Queen Elizabeth (1533-1603). He was born at Hampshire, England, between 5 and 6 P. M., December 14, 1590, and was a Bachelor of Arts of Magdalen College, Oxford.

On Sunday, February 21, 1609/1610, the Reverend William Crashaw, in the Temple, in London, preached a sermon before Lord Delaware, on the eve of his sailing for Virginia, his text being Daniel xii, 3: "They that turn many to righteousness shall shine as the stars forever and ever." It seems that the settlement and colonization of this new domain over which he was going to preside had a strong religious significance as applied to the Indians and their evangelization. In this sermon the minister said:

"Thy ancestor, many hundred years ago, gained great honor to thy house," referring to the capture by Roger de la Warr, assisted by Sir John de Pelham, of the French King, John II, September 19, 1356, at Poictiers, where the English were commanded by the Black Prince. His motto was, in consequence, "Jour de ma vie," in reference to that fortunate day. It is probable, I think, that there was a relationship between the Reverend William Crashaw and Ursula Croshaw, the wife of Colonel John West, the mother of Anne West and the daughter of Major Joseph Croshaw.

The Wests owned Shirley, so named because Thomas West, Lord Delaware, married Cecilly, daughter of Sir Thomas Sherley. They owned, also, Westover, the derivation of whose name is self-evident. On Good

<u>GENERATION TWELVE</u>

Captain John Fox (1626-1682) and
Margaret Thomas (1628-1681)

Captain John was born in Middlesex,
England and died in New Kent, Surry,
VA.

Captain John Fox (b. Abt. 1626, d. April
16, 1682) **Captain John Fox** (son of
John Fox) was born Abt. 1626 in
Steppney Parrish, Middlesex, England,
and died April 16, 1682 in Virginia. He
married **Margaret Thomas** on Abt.
1644 in Suffolk, England.

 Notes for **Captain John Fox**:
He was associated with "other members
of his family in merchant-trader
operations" and was the Captain John
Fox who was commander of the
"William and John" which sailed early
in April, 1659 from England to Virginia.
Early in June, 1659, the "William and
John" sailed from Virginia back to
England with Captain John Fox in
command. The restoration of the Stuarts

(Charles II) to the throne of England was celebrated in Virginia on proclamation of the governor on October 20, 1660. The "John and William" was then in port in Virginia and its commander, Captain John Fox, participated in the occasion. "The York County Levy, October, 1660, included a sum to pay Captain Fox for 6 cases of drams for firing 'his great gunnes.'"

John Fox, Jr. "was the Captain John Fox, Mariner, who on 2 April 1661 married Margaret Thomas in St. Dunstan's Church, Stephney Parish, County Middlesex, England. This evidently was his second marriage."

John Fox, Jr., together with Thomas Lester and Gilbert Thornbrough, were given grants of land in Virginia on September 20, 1661, by King Charles II. He evidently gave up his activities as a sea captain soon after his second marriage and devoted time to business activities in London or its vicinity. The last known record of him in London shows that on October 20, 1663, he was granted administration of the estates of his brother, Stephen Fox.

John Fox, Jr., sailed from Bristol, England, probably in 1664, for Virginia. He doubtless settled on the tract of 1,000 acres granted him by Charles II on September 20, 1661. This land was divided in 1750 between the Reverend John Fox and William Fox and was then described as being situated in Petworth Parish of Gloucester County, Va.

In 1663 he is mentioned as owning land adjoining George Major, Richard Lee, John Chamberlin and John Lewis in Gloucester and New Kent Counties, VA. His son was granted the land which "as son and heir of John Fox", was his right as eldest son. On 16 Aug 1667 Mr. John Lewis was assigned land on both sides of Poropotank Swamp adjoining said Lewis plantation by Old Woman's Point & adjoining Richard Major, Tomoty

Lowdell, George Major, John Fox, Richard Lee, John Chamberlain, to the mill.

Between July 25, 1681, and February 28, 1682/3, John Fox, Jr. brought '200 acres of land lying partly in New Kent County and partly in Gloucester County, Va.' This land was confirmed by grant to John Fox, Jr. on February 28, 1682/3. After the death of John Fox, Jr. it was re-granted on April 16, 1662/3 to Henry Fox 1st.

GENERATION THIRTEEN

John Fox (1602-1665) and Elizabeth Convers (1601-1659)

Born in England and died in Middlesex, England.

GENERATION FOURTEEN

Henry Fox (1578-1625) and Elizabeth Pickernell (1582-1625)

Born in Great Missenden, Buckinghamshire, England. Died in London, England.

GENERATION FIFTEEN

William Fox (1545-1578) and Annie Lane (1563-1578)

Born in St. Dunstan and All Saints, Middlesex, England and Died in Pilkington, Rhodes, Lancashire, England.

GENERATION SIXTEEN

Henry Fox (1521-1545) born in Great Missenden Parish Buckinghamshire, England. Died same place.

Wife is Hawkes Hawess ? 1530-1547

GENERATION SEVENTEEN

William Fox (1497-1558) and _____
Grey

William born in Stewkley,
Buckinghamshire, England and died
same.

Spouse is unknown Grey

The line of William Fox (1497-1559) of
Stewkley Manor in Buckinghamshire
has been traced by one Fox researcher
back to the Norman Invader Robert de
Vaux born about 1010.

GENERATION EIGHTEEN

William Fox (1450-1510) and Elizabeth
(1452)

William was born in St. Dunstan and All
Saints, Middlesex, England

His spouse is Elizabeth unknown

GENERATION NINETEEN

John Vaux Fox (1430-1487)

FOX FAMILY INFORMATION

The ancient family of Fox in England, with branches in America and other countries, is of Norman-French origin. Its name derives from the French word "renard", also spelled "Rreinard" or "reynard" which translated into old Anglo-Saxon (and now modern English) means "fox". The use of surnames was introduced into England by the Norman adventurers under William the Conqueror in 1066, but for centuries was confined to the upper classes; however, such usage became general in Scotland about the twelfth century. Prior to the year 1272 the name "Renard" (etc.) in England had resolved into Fox. (See "The Norman People," page 249-Fox.) Some persons of the name are mentioned in early records, as follows:

In 1148 William Vulpis or Renard held lands from the Bishop of Winchester, in England. The family continued there as le Fox, and from it descended the Earls of Ilchester and Lords Holland.Robert Reinard (F0x) was in Normandy (in France) in 1198.

Aelix and Ranulph Renouard were in England in 1199.

Gilbert le Fox and others of the name were in England in 1272.

Turstain Renouard was in England during the time of King Henry IV (1367-1413).

At an early date not yet determined, one branch of the Fox family settled in Buckinghamshire (Bucks County, or County Bucks), England. Persons of the name who are mentioned in Lipscomb's "History of Buckinghamshire" were:

John Fox, LLB, Rector of Hedsor Parish, Desborough Hundred, from 16 December 1457 to 16 August 1459. - (Vol. 3, p. 580).

Thomas Fox, Rector of Maids' Moreton Parish, Buckingham Hundred, during 1503-531. - (Vol. 3, p. 43.)

John Fox, Abbot of Great Missenden Parish, Aylesbury Hundred, from 21 November 1528 to about 1538. On 5 September 1534 he subscribed to the King's Supremacy, under Seal. - (Vol. 2, p. 368.) He probably was an uncle of the first known Henry Fox of Great Missenden, and later might have been Vicar of Stewekley Parish.

John Fox, Vicar of Stewkley Parish, Cotteslow Hundred, from 10 December 1545 to 4 July 1554 and from 1559/60 until the time of his death shortly before 10 April 1583. - (Vol. 3, p. 472-3.) Some historians have erroneously identified him as John Foxe the Martyrologist who died on 15 April 1587. He formerly might have been Abbot of Great Missenden Parish. The Stewkley Parish Registers (1545-1653) contain entries relating to members of the Fox family, which persons might have been his children and grandchildren (baptized during the years of 1552-1588). He probably married in 1551 after celibacy of the clergy was rejected by the Church of England under the Reformed Faith.

(Copied from BE THEY REMEMBERED, p. 73-74, written by Craig Smith.)

Sources

ancestry.com

wikipedia.com